Discite benefacere

Learn to do good.

Isaiah 1:17

Leaders shed light

or

impose darkness.

"*I am delighted and honored to commend Chuck Ferguson's book on leadership because I have seen these principles at play in his own life. Chuck epitomizes good leadership in a hundred different ways, often at great personal cost, and I count myself as one of the happy beneficiaries.*"

■ ANGUS M. GUNN
Professor, University of British Columbia

"*Sometimes the simplest message is the biggest message. This is one of those times.*"

■ ROGER LOOYENGA
CEO, Auto-Owners Insurance

"Indomitable Spirit *gives real-life examples for the leader who wants to leave a legacy beyond the bottom line in the lives of employees and customers. I have known Chuck for thirty years and have observed how he consistently inspires people (including me) to focus on value-driven principles that produce enduring influence in all our relationships.*"

■ RICK MALOUF
Principal, Acacia Capital

INDOMITABLE
SPIRIT

Chuck Ferguson
Steve Duin

INDOMITABLE SPIRIT
published by Agora Publishing
P.O. Box 82033
Portland, Oregon 97282-0033
© 2004 by Chuck Ferguson

International Standard Book Number: 0-9708257-1-4

Cover design by Gary Tompkins, Sisters, Oregon
Cover photos by Kevin Barry Studios
Interior design and typeset by Katherine Lloyd, Bend, Oregon

Unless otherwise indicated, Scripture quotations are from:
The Holy Bible, New King James Version
© 1982 by Thomas Nelson, Inc.

The Holy Bible, New International Version (NIV)
© 1973, 1984 by International Bible Society
Used by permission of Zondervan Publishing House

Printed in the United States of America

04 05 06 07 08—10 9 8 7 6 5 4 3 2 1

For
CHELSEA ANN

You spoke to me clearly,
simply, and with breathtaking
insight beyond your years
about leaders and leadership.
I love you,
Papa

Table of Contents

A Personal Preface

I crawled out of bed early one spring morning, leaving myself barely enough time to prepare for a meeting of the YMCA Board of Management. I was hurriedly reviewing the agenda—membership, financials, program evaluations—when I happened to glance at the faded logo on my rugged ol' coffee cup:

INSPIRE GREATNESS
Special Olympics

What a wake-up call. That is the crux of leadership: to inspire greatness in the people we live and work with each and every day.

Leading people is hard work. It's messy and intensely personal. It is a mission that involves tensions, failures, trade-offs, celebrations, and disappointments. But done well, it is a ministry of incredible rewards.

When it is done well, all the stakeholders—the customers, employees, families, shareholders, community, and yes, even the "bottom line"—benefit greatly.

This small but proud book on leaders and leadership is not an academic or historical study. There are no quick fixes, no how-tos, and no "Go get 'ems!" We don't even offer much in the way of technique or skills.

Instead, this book will challenge you to dig deep. To get visceral and take a look at your inner life, because that's where greatness is born!

I believe leadership is, at its best, for everyone. Leadership is the cornerstone of all that we do as part of a family, a business, a community.

I want to leave you with a practical thought or two:

Because leadership is about people and relationships, get involved with the people around you.

Each time you plunge into this book, pick out a thought about leadership that you can put into practice when you leave the book behind.

Include a thought about leadership whenever you deliver a memo, a speech, or a thank-you note.

Share these thoughts on leadership with your family and your friends at work. Use words only if they become necessary. *13*

Finally, rewrite this little book one chapter at a time with your own life story.

Enjoy the Leadership Journey!

■ CHUCK FERGUSON
Lake Oswego, Oregon
March 2004

Foreword
by Bob Farrell

D uring one of the most memorable weeks of my life, two dramatic things happened: I discovered Young Life…and I met Chuck Ferguson.

Late in the summer of 1972, I was invited up to the Malibu Club, a Young Life property in Canada, as an adult guest. I knew very little about Young Life at the time. My expectations were pretty low. I was expecting a typical church camp. Deadly serious. Nobody having any fun.

It didn't work out that way. Over the course of that week, I experienced the most effective presentation of the gospel to teenagers that I've ever seen. I was surrounded by three hundred kids who, during the daylight hours, had the time of their lives, sailing, swimming, and waterskiing in one of the prettiest spots on earth.

And every night, we all sat down together, sang a few songs and listened to the words of a Canadian who sought to describe the person of Jesus Christ.

That guy was Chuck Ferguson.

Thirty-two years later, I'm still involved with Young Life and I'm still friends with Chuck. He was more than the camp speaker that week back in '72. He was the camp manager, involved in everything the kids were doing, from the morning calisthenics all the way through the midnight swim. Because those kids had fun with him all day, they were ready to listen when he got up to speak each night and got serious about life.

As they say in Young Life, Chuck earned the right to be heard.

He was absolutely genuine. He never tried to draw attention to himself, like so many people do. He was calm and solid and spoke the truth. Everything he said was from the heart.

Since leaving Young Life, Chuck Ferguson has been speaking to various business groups on the subject of leadership.

Each time I've recommended him to an organization, some-one from that company has written or called me to say thanks. Every time.

Once again, Chuck has earned the right to be heard. His current job at Norpac Food Sales began with a speech on leadership. The executives were so impressed that they asked him to come on board and counsel them on a daily basis.

This is not a long book, but it packs a heck of a punch. And it's pure Chuck. He understands the nature of true leadership. Honesty. Sincerity. Taking the time to say thank you. Becoming a servant. When Chuck writes about serving one another, I can hear the echoes of the talks he gave thirty-two summers ago at Malibu. That is, after all, the message of the Bible: We are here to serve.

I am convinced you will be well served by the chapters that follow. What Chuck doesn't know about leadership, it turns out, his granddaughter does. I can't recommend this book highly enough. Dive in now. You can thank me later.

■ BOB FARRELL
Cofounder, Farrell's and Stanford's Restaurants

Foreword
by Dr. Peter Legge

I have known Chuck Ferguson for thirty years. We served the mission of Young Life in Canada together during a memorable period of our lives.

I have heard Chuck speak dozens of times and heard him say, "Leadership is never given. Leadership is always recognized."

As a father, husband, grandfather, leader, and founder of the 21st Century Leadership Group, he does just that:

Lead.

This, his first book on leadership, provides an honest, straight-forward, no-nonsense approach to the need for strong leaders in our world: at home, in the workplace, in our schools and churches, just about everywhere!

He speaks of character, integrity, and a servant's spirit to be at the very heart of leadership in our community.

His eight-year-old granddaughter, Chelsea, eloquently hits the nail on the head when she says, "Leaders always tell the truth." Out of the mouths of babes comes wisdom.

And out of the mouth of Chuck comes the truth we all need to hear and read again about ourselves and our leadership style.

This book is a must-read for you and your staff. You will learn from Chuck Ferguson. I have. I do. I will.

■ Dr. Peter Legge, LL.D. (Hon)
Publisher, Author, Professional Speaker

CHAPTER 1

Shadow

*Leadership, besides being a great
creative force, can be diabolical.*

AGATHA CHRISTIE
Passenger to Frankfurt

*And David shepherded
them with integrity of heart;
with skillful hands, he led them.*

PSALM 78:72

Where, oh where, are the leaders?

Managers? We've got a million of 'em. Baseball managers. Floor managers. Crisis managers. Business and management classes. Ask Warren Bennis, who once taught at the University of Southern California: "America and its business community," Bennis said, "have been managed to the point of ruin."

Managers? Managers we've got. We're surrounded. But leaders? "We're in desperate need of leaders," Bennis said. "Unfortunately, it is increasingly difficult to find men and women of vision who are willing to stand on principle and make their voices heard.

"One has to wonder, where have all the leaders gone?"

22 Where are the leaders? No one seems to know. Read the headlines. Listen to the news. While running for president in 2000, George W. Bush campaigned on the theme, "It is a time for new beginnings and new leadership."

As a half-dozen Democrats got in line to oppose the president in 2004, that clarion call was sounded time and again. Howard Dean insisted in January, "We can regain the moral leadership of this country…by having a foreign policy based on cooperation, not confrontation, and we will." When Wesley Clark dropped out of the race in February, he joked that his campaign came out of the starting blocks with "no money, no staff, no position papers, and a candidate with no political experience. All we really had was hope, a lifetime of experience in leadership, and a vision for America."

And when the *New York Times* reflected on the similar backgrounds—including membership in secret societies—of the incumbent and his Democratic challenger, Senator John Kerry of Massachusetts, the newspaper noted, "The larger question is whether Skull and Bones inculcated values of leadership—or, put another way, a sense of entitlement—in Mr. Kerry and Mr. Bush, beyond what was already driven home by Yale."

23

Countless other commentators recognized the value of leadership. Thomas Friedman, a columnist for the *Times,* argues that the Palestinians need their own state "and a new leadership." An editorial board insists that only "new leadership" will succeed in getting a Patients' Bill of Rights through Congress. And as I write this, lawmakers in Washington are thrilled about new leadership at the SEC.

Have you ever heard a politician say, "We need a new kind of management in Washington, D.C."? Not even Ross Perot tried to run on that platform.

No, leaders and leadership are what's missing. In your local school district. In the circles of local government. In the church and synagogue. In the business community. In the world of the nonprofits.

Especially in the business community. It's difficult to exaggerate the devastating impact—not only on Wall Street, but on the street where you live—of the collapse of such companies as Enron, Arthur Andersen, Global Crossing, and MCI-WorldCom.

The courts are still trying to calculate the depth and breadth of the fraud these companies perpetuated on the financial markets. In June 2002, officials at MCI-WorldCom admitted the company had hidden almost $4 billion in costs, which prompted the largest bankruptcy filing in U.S. history. In a civil lawsuit, the Securities and Exchange Commission said that an accounting scheme "directed and approved by WorldCom's senior management" allowed MCI-WorldCom to fraudulently report 2001 cash flow of $2.4 billion, rather than its actual loss of $662 million.

MCI-WorldCom's accounting firm was Arthur Andersen. That firm also did the math for Enron, collecting $25 million in auditing fees and $27 million in consulting fees in 2001.

That was enough, apparently, to look the other way while Enron phonied up its balance sheets.

Then there's Global Crossing. The telecommunications giant made Gary Winnick, the man who launched the firm, a $6 billion man. While the boom was on, the company grew from five employees to a telecom giant of ten thousand…but when the bubble burst, many of those employees were given three days' notice that their health benefits were being cut off. They were denied severance pay. Many had to sell their homes. Their pension funds, a product of their faith and trust in the company for which they worked, were ruined.

Gary Winnick was not similarly distressed. Even as Global Crossing rolled toward bankruptcy court and the fourth largest insolvency in U.S. history, Winnick was buying and *bulldozing* a $16-million estate overlooking the Bel-Air Country Club in Los Angeles, just to ensure that he had all the room he needed to construct his personal dream house, a shy little cottage with a $94 million price tag.

Where are the leaders? Do you think they are ensconced in

25

$94 million mansions? Are they driven by the "values of leadership?" Or, to put it another away, are they energized by nothing more than a sense of entitlement?

We might want to ask the man lathering up behind $6,000 shower curtains, Tyco's Dennis Kozlowski. Kozlowski was lauded by *Business Week* as the country's "Most Aggressive CEO" in a 2001 cover story—a story, by the way, that came out less than a year before the company's stock plunged 75 percent and the investors so charmed by his leadership lost $92 billion. Even as Tyco closed or consolidated three hundred plants and laid off eleven thousand workers, Arianna Huffington writes in *Pigs at the Trough* that Kozlowski earned $466 million in salary, bonuses, and perks in his last three years on the payroll.

Is that what leadership has come to? Pigs at the trough? Is that where our "leaders" are going, marching out of their corporate offices in handcuffs?

In his book *Managing People Is Like Herding Cats,* Warren Bennis reminds us:

Once upon a time, we all wanted to be Lindbergh or DiMaggio or Astaire, because they were the best at what they did; now we want to be Pickens, Trump or Iacocca, because they're rich. Far too often now, our idols are all smoke and mirrors, sound and fury, signifying nothing.

Think about these men and women. Think about the roles of these mega-rich idols in a perplexingly unique phenomenon in this country's history. These people had it all. They had security. They didn't have to worry about paying for their kids' college education or the brand-new Lexus. They could travel. They could lavish thousands of dollars upon their favorite charity. They had deep pockets. Before the accounting firm began shredding documents and credibility, money was never an issue at Arthur Andersen. If you worked at Arthur Andersen, you never had to worry about taking home a laptop. A laptop? Absolutely! Take two. Store one at the beach house.

Money wasn't the issue at Arthur Andersen, Enron, MCI-WorldCom, or any of these companies. At one point, Gary Winnick was trying to recruit a guy named Thomas Casey to come work for him.

This is how Winnick described that hiring:

> *I said, "Tom what does it take?"*
>
> *He says, "Gary, I'm going to throw out a number. It'll never happen."*
>
> *"Give me a number, Tom."*
>
> *"Twenty million."*
>
> *I say, "When can you start? I'll write the check." Insurance! You want to be a leader, you've got to be bold. You've got to step up to the plate.*

No kidding? Is that what leadership is all about? "You want to be a leader, you've got to be bold. You've got to step up to the plate." You've got to be tough, even if that means climbing over people. Is that what we're missing? Is a lack of boldness behind this persistent crisis in leadership?

Or is it something else? Is it possible this crisis may have more to do with the fact that when Global Crossing announced plans to lay off two thousand employees in August 2001, it made a different arrangement with ol' Tom Casey. Even as two thousand people lost their jobs, the *NewsHour with Jim Lehrer* reported, the company "wiped out the terms of an $8 million loan to then-CEO Thomas Casey, in effect providing Casey with an $8 million gift."

In the debate over leadership, Gary Winnick and Tom Casey are part of the problem. If you'll read on, we can start moving toward the solution.

29

CHAPTER 2

Heart

*Use power to help people. For we are given power
not to advance our own purposes nor to make a great
show in the world, nor a name. There is but one use
of power and it is to serve people.*

GEORGE H. W. BUSH

*Leadership is a potent combination
of strategy and character. But if you must be
without one, be without the strategy.*

GEN. H. NORMAN SCHWARZKOPF

Agreed. But let's talk a little strategy. I can't sum up
leadership in five words or less. Leadership is
about a lot of things. But when we survey the
arrogant wreckage of these corporate giants, I hope we can
agree on this:

In its simplest and most powerful form, leadership is about people and the intimate, intricate relationships between them. It's about core values. And it's about being connected, for the benefit of all, in a community.

Far too many of us have grown up thinking leadership involves a position. It's not about position. A title doesn't make you a leader. I know you've heard people say, "I love my job, but I can't stand the person I work for."

Why? Because position or titles do not automatically inspire leadership. Position is vague and external. And leadership, I've come to believe, is personal and internal. It has its roots deep inside each one of us.

I've come quite a ways, I might add. For me, leadership has been a journey. I haven't reached this point armed with—or guided by—clichés and anecdotes. Yes, there are people, wonderful books, and experiences that have shaped my life. I'm still benefiting from the counsel and the experience of friends. But there is no simple answer to our questions about the nature of leadership. I don't have a toolbox or a quick ten-step seminar. I'm not a quote machine. And I'm still learning, each and every day, from my mistakes and from the wonderful people that cross my path.

During the first thirty years, I toiled in the business and nonprofit world. I was heavy handed. Very top down. I drove to the top because I believed leadership resided at the top. I flat walked over people. A good friend of mine named Jim Lussier—whom you will hear more about later—once told me, "When I was a little kid, I hated bullies. Then I became one. That's how I ran the hospital. I pushed and pushed." Let me tell you: I recognized my reflection in the mirror he held up.

There is a time in each of our lives when we have to make a decision about leadership.

For many of us, it's a conversion experience. We *were* something…and then we learned that leadership is something quite different than what we had imagined or experienced. The quest to understand just how different is an inside-out journey. And at a crucial juncture in that journey we discover that leadership is not so much about what we do.

It's about who we are. That can be a painful revelation. Few of us like to inquire within. We're a little edgy about probing deep inside. We're a tad nervous about confronting the character we bring to moments of great crisis and utter loneliness. But that's what we need to do if we want to tap our capacity for leadership.

When I was a senior at Grant High School in Portland, Oregon, still fumbling around at the edges of what I wanted to do and who I wanted to be, the SAT tests were just becoming a big deal. It was 1958, and I remember the SATs fairly well because I was advised not to take them.

"You're not college material," they said. "Maybe, just maybe, you might want to look for the kind of job that doesn't require you go to college."

That's not the sort of advice that does a lot for a kid, but it was performance-based…and like a lot of kids in that era, I was judged on performance.

I went out for the track team at Grant. I figured, *Well, while I'm not doing that great in school, at least I can pole-vault.* As it turned out, I could pole-vault with the best of 'em. I won school meets, city meets, the state meet. I was in my element charging down that lane, planting that pole, and following it up into the air. I was a winner. I was parked in first place.

Those were special yet anxious times. I was competing; I was performing; I was submitting myself to be judged on how high I could jump. I needed someone to validate the results, and the guy who showed up was a coach named Denny Sullivan. He understood the motivational power of leadership. He believed in me. He challenged me and he celebrated with me.

He wasn't the only one at Grant High School who believed in me. I remember my speech teacher, Opal Hamilton. We met in homeroom. You remember homeroom? Taking roll. Spitballs in the back of the neck. Copying homework. Opal Hamilton ruled my homeroom at Grant, and there came a time when she convinced me to enroll in her speech class.

I remember the first time we had to stumble up to the front of her class and deliver a one-minute speech. I don't remember ever walking back to my seat, but I got through it. Then there was the two-minute speech and the three-minute speech and those "speech meets." I began winning them. I don't think any of my high school buddies ever noticed, but Ms. Hamilton was always there in the wings.

She was there when I beat our student body president my senior year and won the Oregon State Knights of Pythias contest. That was special. Ms. Hamilton came up to me after the speech while I was still hobnobbing with the judges.

She was about so big; she didn't even come up to my chin. Had a bun in the back of her hair. "You did a great job, Chuck," she said. "Could I see your speech for a minute?"

So, I handed it to her—a seven-minute speech, carefully written out, word for word. I'm sure I puffed out my chest a little. I was probably trying to figure out where she was hiding the frame she was going to wrap around it.

But as she was talking to me, and other people were talking to me, Ms. Hamilton began to tear that speech up. She tore the pages in half, then took the two halves and tore them again.

I was staring at her. My mouth was hanging open. I was thinking, *What the heck is going on?* I wanted to keep that speech. I mean, I'd just won the Knights of Pythias with it. And there she was tearing it up.

Of course, only then did she put an exclamation point on the statement she was making about leadership. She put her finger on my chest, poking me square on the breastbone, right above the heart, and said, "Chuck, you were good today. But don't ever give that speech again unless it comes straight out of your heart. Then, you'll be great."

37

That's where greatness resides. That's where leadership begins. On the inside. That's where the passion is. That's what you uncover when you're finally ready to dig down deep.

Inside

It is only with the heart that one can see rightly:
What is essential is invisible to the eye.

ANTOINE DE ST. EXUPERY

The more faithfully you listen to the voice within you,
the better you will hear what is sounding outside.

DAG HAMMARSKJOLD

A friend of mine was in Ocean City, New Jersey, several years ago. Ocean City is the antithesis of Atlantic City, a collection of grand, glowing casinos and dreary city blocks thirty miles or so up the coast. Atlantic City is wet, slick and wild. Ocean City is dry. You have to leave town to buy a bottle of scotch or the gin to splash in your tonic. Ocean City is a great place for families to spend a week at The Shore, and the town revolves around a board-walk that stretches for twenty-three or twenty-four blocks.

This friend of mine was relaxing on the boardwalk during his lunch hour, enjoying the fresh air. That's when he noticed a little girl walking toward him, trailing her mother. She had both hands wrapped around a paper cone capped by a great pink stack of cotton candy.

40

I once made a mistake with cotton candy. I let our daughters carry some into the backseat of our car. Ten minutes later, it was everywhere. In their pig tails. Jammed up their nose. I finally had to sell that car. There's not much you can do when the upholstery is lacquered in cotton candy.

But here was my friend and here came that little girl. She couldn't have been much more than eight or nine years old. As she passed by, my friend leaned down and said to her, "Little girl, how can someone as tiny as you eat all that cotton candy?"

Without missing a step, the little girl looked up at him and said, "Mister, I'm a whole lot bigger on the inside than I am on the outside."

You want a definition for leadership? Well, let's start right there:

> *Leadership is about being a whole lot bigger on the inside than we are on the outside.*

Inside, after all, is where we store our core values. *Inside* is where we maintain our dignity, where we harbor our capacity for compassion. *Inside* is the good earth in which everything we show to the outside world has taken root.

41

And what's *inside* drives my behavior. Crafts my thought life. Shapes my words. Defines my relationships. Determines how I value myself and others. And influences my decisions.

Don't assume that what's *inside* is transparent and accessible to those on the outside. Michelangelo once said that the perfect form lies concealed in the block of stone; all that is necessary is to chip away until it's revealed. That's a great insight. Get those rock hammers ready.

And don't forget that the delicate fabric between what exists on the inside and what we confront on the outside can be very thin. I don't think you can work for a company if its core values don't line up with your core values. You can't lead a company—or be led by one—that doesn't believe the same things you do.

In all likelihood, you spend more time at work than you do with your family or curled up in bed. I don't want to suggest that your job is where the best and worst parts of you are on display. But given the time you invest in work, shouldn't your job be the place where your entire personality—and every part of you—is welcome?

Shortly after Henry Ford created the first assembly line for Ford Motor Company, I understand he looked out over the shop floor and said, "Why do I get the whole person when all I want to hire is a pair of hands?"

Maybe because they're attached, Henry! In the twenty-first century, you can't hire a simple pair of hands. You hire "whole" people, and they bring it all to work.

When I turned sixteen, I got my first job. I was hired at a

place called Yaw's Top Notch on the east side of Portland. We used to hang out at the drive-in after school, and I got to know the manager. On my first day of work, an afternoon shift, the manager said, "Chuck, two things to get you started. First, we're thrilled you're here. Second, leave your private life out in the parking lot. When you come to work, you're on our time, not your time."

You cannot say that to people today. "Leave your private life in the parking lot." That's not possible.

Not long ago, I was called into a doctor's office after a routine colonoscopy. This tough and exceedingly kind man said to me, "Chuck, your colonoscopy is showing a tumor that is full of cancer."

If you've ever heard that kind of diagnosis, I'm sure you know how hard that hit me. I was staggered. Almost everything in my life changed. Drastically. Immediately. Without wasting any time, I had to go in for cancer surgery on my colon. I don't think I need to tell you that tumor was on my mind in the weeks leading up to the surgery. No one could ask me to leave that cancer in the parking lot.

When one out of every two marriages ends in divorce, when both parents are working and leaving the latchkey out for the kids coming home from school, when the economy is down and drug use is up, you can't ask your employees to check their private life at the door.

A leader has no choice but to see the whole person. "All politics," U.S. Senator Mark Hatfield of Oregon once said to *44* me, "are relational. And that is also the heart of leadership." Deep, vital relationships aren't possible unless you're willing to deal with the whole person, in the context of the core values that you share. Those core values create the culture of your business, and that culture is what people remember.

How I wish our average board of directors took more seriously the responsibility to defend those values and that culture. Down at the corner grocery store or the local dry cleaner, business is utterly dependent on the connection you make with the customer across the counter. But in large, complex organizations—companies that show a hundred different faces to the public—the directors are the face of an organization and its conscience. They are the gatekeepers of a company's mission and its vision.

Just as leaders need to grapple with the whole person, boards are responsible for maintaining healthy relationships inside the entire organization...*and* responsible for the core values that connect a company to the world outside its walls. They have the standing, if I may borrow that legal term, to both challenge and encourage the salesmen and the CEOs. And you better believe that the fate of the companies I talked about in the opening chapter would have been markedly different if a few more directors had stood tall instead of ducking out of the way.

45

We are shielded by what we show on the outside and motivated by who we are on the inside. I encourage you to commit yourself to making your hidden beliefs obvious. You must first become the leader that you yearn to see in the people around you.

CHAPTER 4

Caregiver

*Opportunity is missed by most people
because it is dressed in overalls
and looks like work.*

THOMAS A. EDISON

*Men occasionally stumble on the truth,
but most of them pick themselves up and hurry off
as if nothing had happened.*

WINSTON CHURCHILL

My favorite quote about leadership comes courtesy of a gentleman—an absolute gentleman—named Max DePree. Max is the former CEO and chairman of the Herman Miller Company, a second- or third-generation Fortune 100 company that builds some of the finest office furniture in the world.

This is what Max had to say about leadership in a book entitled *Leadership Is an Art:*

> *The first responsibility of a leader is to define reality.*
> *The last is to say thank you. In between the two, the*
> *leader must become a servant...*

There are three parts to Max's quote: defining reality, saying thank you, becoming a servant. I'd describe each of them, one at a time, if all three weren't embodied in the story of a man named Jim Lussier.

I first met Jim on the cover of *Oregon Business* magazine. In the summer of 1998, this fifty-something guy in a blue blazer with curly salt-and-pepper hair popped up on the magazine cover beside the words "Say Goodbye to the S.O.B." Below that banner was a small explanatory deck: "When old-style management doesn't work."

Lussier was the CEO of St. Charles Medical Center in Bend. I was so impressed with his story that I wrote him a note. Within a week, I was driving over to Central Oregon to see him and to speak with him about his leadership journey.

Lussier was ex-military with an MBA. For twenty-two years, he ran his hospital like he once ran his unit: command and control. When Jim said "Jump," his fifty-two managers jumped higher than he asked them to because that's how you got promoted at St. Charles. That's how you got more money. You jumped. You lunged at the carrot.

The organizational charters at St. Charles were pretty clear: Jim was the commander in chief. He was comfortable with the bureaucracy he had inherited. It was reasonably successful. It was traditional, always focused on the bottom line. It was authoritarian, and he was the authority.

Back in 1992, Jim picked up several books on leadership. Now, that started a transformation in his thinking that could have been trouble. In *Heroic Leadership,* a book on what we can learn about leadership from the four hundred-year history of the Jesuits, Chris Lowney notes that in recent years:

> *The very notion of leadership has progressively been hijacked by corporate-speak. Corporate managers and their consultants or academic advisers are those most obsessed with the leadership gap. And the corporate*

work force is the greatest consumer of leadership litera-
ture. So it's no surprise that it's written in terms that
appeal to a corporate audience. And what appeals to
corporate America? Let's be honest. All our claims
about our enlightened, inclusive business sensibilities
notwithstanding, U.S. corporate culture remains a
towel-snapping, take-no-prisoners macho arena. Is it
really that shocking, then, that our leadership role
models strut forward flashing macho credentials?
Heading the guru list by a wide, wide margin are the
sports coaches and superstars: Pat Riley, Phil Jackson,
Coach K, Joe Torre and so on. Trailing not far behind
are the military leaders: Sun Tzu, Attila, Patton,
Ulysses S. Grant, Robert E. Lee and on and on.

Jim Lussier, in other words, could have easily picked up a
book that celebrated his macho, authoritarian, I-am-the-
biggest-SOB-in-the-valley instincts. Fortunately, he didn't.
Instead, he started attending conferences on leadership, and
he heard people like me suggest that leadership, might have
a lot less to do with telling people to jump and a lot more to
do with lifting them up.

So it came to pass that Jim walked into St. Charles one morning and took a long look at the 1,100 people who, by and large, had worked for him for the last twenty-two years. Standing there at the front doors of the hospital, Jim decided that he worked for 1,100 people. They didn't work for him.

They didn't have one pain-in-the-neck boss. *He* had 1,100 bosses.

The first definition of a leader is to define reality. If you're a manager, you're under the impression that people work for you. If you're a leader, you work for them…because you're there to help make them successful.

Lussier gathered his team around him. He tried to explain the transformation in his thinking. He probably told his management team what he told the writer for *Oregon Business,* that the hospital needed to focus on the patient as a customer.

As he said in the magazine, "Would you go into Nordstrom if the first thing they did was stick you in a waiting room and say, 'I'll be back in an hour'?"

His managers thought he was going through a midlife crisis, that the following morning he'd probably show up with a Harley and gold chains around his neck. They thought he'd gone wacko. Do you know what he wanted to do? He wanted to collect the 1,100 name tags people in the hospital wore and remove the titles. No more "CEO." No more "Head Surgeon, Neurology." No more "Lead RN, Pediatrics."

52 Just their names. What description was supposed to go under the name? Well, Jim asked, what business are we in? Are we in the business of being "head surgeons"? Are we in the business of being the CEO? No? Well, what *is* our business?

Caregiving.

That's what they finally figured out. And that's why if you show up at St. Charles tomorrow, you'll meet Jim Lussier or Suzie Smith or Jim Johnson, and their name tags all announce the same thing: "Caregiver."

The folks who sweep the floors and mop up ER? Caregiver. The people answering 911? Caregiver.

The janitors? You know, there's a wonderful quote from Royal Alcott: "Leadership," he insists, "is the initiation and direction of endeavor in the pursuit of consequence. Anything else is criticism from janitors."

But at St. Charles, janitors—critical and otherwise—have a part to play in the hospital's mission. They may be behind the curtains rather than at the front of the stage, but the title on their name tag is just the same as the pediatric cardiologists:

Caregiver.

Why? Because the reality of St. Charles, Jim Lussier decided, is that those name tags shouldn't assert your *status* but define your *service*.

Jim's next decision was that the hospital staff needed to begin listening to patients and their families.

This is, generally, anathema to the medical community. Doctors don't make a habit of listening to patients. They are used to dictating to patients and—let's be honest—ordering them around. When a doctor asks how you're feeling, look out: He's warming up to tell you just how wrong you are.

Jim Lussier had a better idea. You know what the staff at St. Charles found out when they began listening to their patients? First off, they discovered that the patients hated those nightgowns you have to wear.

54 There's no great mystery as to why. Your butt hangs out in the back. Big time. When I went in for my colon surgery, the nurse threw one of those nightgowns on the bed and said, "Put this on and I'll be back." When I got it on, I was hanging out in the back, so I thought, *Well, I've got it on the wrong way*. You've been there, haven't you? So, I turned the gown around and put it in on the other way. Not a pretty picture.

In hotels around America, there's a perennial problem with people swiping those plush white bathrobes. I can guarantee you this: There's no theft problem with your average hospital nightgowns. They're uncomfortable. They're humiliating. St. Charles Medical Center is over one hundred years old, and they've never lost a single one.

That's why they're no longer the standard uniform at the St. Charles. Since Jim Lussier decided to shake up the place, St. Charles has allowed patients to wear whatever they want. Nighties, pajamas, a running suit: If you bring it, you can wear it.

Why? Because it's about the patient at St. Charles, not about some tired, irrelevant habits. Leadership demands that you listen to the people who drive your business. You don't tell your customers what to wear when they're facing a traumatic, unpredictable experience in your hospital. You listen carefully as your customers tell you what makes them comfortable. You remain still while they explain their needs.

You also listen to what they have to tell you about the food. When I drove over to Bend, I reached the hospital thirty minutes early, so Jim's assistant, Patsy, said, "Chuck, why don't you head down the hall to the dining room and grab a cup of coffee? Jim will see you there at nine o'clock."

So I took her advice. I headed down the hall, and I'm thinking, *This is great. I'm on the second floor. It's the executive suite and the executives have their own dining room.* That's par for the course in the corporate world, right? They have their own elevator. They have their own dining room.

When I got there, the room had plush carpet, fresh flowers on the tables, and beautiful music on the sound system. That's about the time I noticed there were little kids running around and a box of Kleenex on every table. And I figured out this was the hospital cafeteria after all.

Now, I've been in quite a few hospital dining rooms. I think this is the first one that didn't smother my appetite the second I walked through the door. There wasn't a linoleum floor, nor a small armada of those gagging Styrofoam cups. When I went looking for a cup, all I could find was a china mug and a giant pot of Starbucks.

Not some freeze-dried instant. Starbucks! It smelled great, but when I put my $1.50 on the counter, the lady behind the register said, "Sir, while you're in our hospital, you are our guest. Coffee, tea, and iced tea are all a gift from us to you."

The first responsibility of a leader is to define reality. The last is to say thank you. Do I need to explain the Kleenex box on every table? Do you know how the hospital figured that out? They listened to their customers, their patients, and the families of their patients.

Management rarely does that. Managers are convinced they have all the answers. Leaders, on the other hand, have the right amount of humility. Leaders have a proper sense of empathy. Leaders have figured out that between defining reality and saying thank you, their job is to be servants to the people who come to them and help them design their business.

57

After listening to those people, Jim Lussier hired the head chef from Ritz Carlton in the hotel chain's Western division to teach his staff how to prepare food. That chef came along and said, "You've heard of our room service? Why not institute it in the hospital? Why not cook each patient's meal precisely the way they want it and send it to them exactly when they want it?"

Why not? Because with all that variety and that cook-to-order timetable, your food costs would go through the roof, right? On the contrary, Jim said, they're *plummeting*…because the patients actually like what they're being served. The hospital is no longer dumping the meals that no one ordered and no one will eat.

Allow me one more story about St. Charles to drive the point home. Fear plays a dramatic part in most hospital experiences. You're afraid something is going to go wrong. The surgeon is going to stumble upon the unexpected. The anesthesiologist is going to make that rare mistake.

The best antidote to this disabling fear? Taking those warm, human hands out of your pocket and laying them on the patient. Willfully. Purposefully. If you go to St. Charles tomorrow, you'll get a twenty-minute massage before your surgery.

In all honesty, many of the doctors and nurses at St. Charles were tentative about this hands-on approach. They weren't trained as massage therapists. They weren't prepared for this revolution in leadership to roll over the culture of the hospital. But they discovered soon enough that their wisdom and their experience and their expertise didn't have the same impact on their customers as their sense of touch did.

People often tell me that leadership is the soft side of business. The poetry. The fluff. The real, vital aspect of business, they insist, is driving sales and product.

I invariably nod my head. I try to be polite as I tell them they're flat-out wrong. St. Charles didn't have a six-month review or a five-year plan. For all I know, they were as surprised as anyone when they began to chart the unexpected changes at the hospital. They noticed, for example, *59* that the amount of anesthetic a patient needed dropped after he or she was given a massage. They noticed that after all that hands-on treatment, patients came out of the operating room and spent less time in post-op.

And they noticed that all the costs of anesthesia and post-op dropped dramatically, dropped to the bottom line.

Don't tell me that leadership doesn't affect the bottom line. Leadership drives the bottom line. When you listen to people, when you take them seriously, when you honor relationships and live out a set of core values...

That drives the bottom line.

CHAPTER 5

Chelsea

Great leadership is a product of character,
of matters like loyalty, sacrifice, endurance, and courage.
WINSTON CHURCHILL

"It's all right!" shouted Aslan joyously. "Once the feet
are put right, all the rest of him will follow."
C. S. LEWIS
The Lion, the Witch and the Wardrobe

I n recent years, I've been on the board of directors at
Norpac Food Sales, the exclusive sales agency for the co-op
that packages and sells frozen vegetables and fruit for 260
farmers in Oregon's Willamette Valley. In January 2003, I was
asked to supervise the in-house operations for Norpac Food
Sales. On the very first day in that position, I met a woman

named Faye who had recently been diagnosed with an advanced stage of breast cancer.

As you can imagine, Faye's prospects weren't very good. She was going through chemotherapy and radiation. And to make matters worse, the person I'd replaced at Norpac had told Faye that the company was dividing up her workload, transferring the responsibility for her accounts and her customers to a variety of other employees.

The implication was clear: "Sorry, Faye, but you're not going to be with us much longer. You have our deepest sympathy, but business is business, and I'm sure you understand, and…"

Faye had been with Norpac Food Sales for forty years. Straight-away, I sat down with her and her team leader in a room and said, "Faye, this is what I've heard about you. Is this what you understand to be true?"

"Yes," she said, tears rolling down her cheeks. As she told me her story, I pulled out the box of Kleenex—thank you, Jim Lussier—and handed it to her. Then I listened to her story.

This is how I responded to it:

"Faye, you don't know me. I've only been in this position for several hours, but I'm only in this position because I know what this company is all about and what you've added to it. You've taken care of us for forty years. Well, now we're going to take care of you. Even if you quit tomorrow, we will pay you until you reach retirement age. Oh, and by the way: I love your wig. And I hear you have a red wig, which I can't wait to see."

That box of Kleenex came in fairly handy over the next several minutes. And Faye has come to work every day since and given Norpac every ounce of her energy. Whenever she has to miss a day because of her chemotherapy, we're there at her desk, covering every one of her customers. On Fridays, she wears the red wig.

What else could we do? What else would you do or have your company do for you? Caring for your people, treating people with kindness and dignity, is often a small thing, but I remember what C. S. Lewis, the great British theologian, once said: Every decision we make, no matter how small, turns us into a more hellish creature or a more heavenly creature.

Leadership is about incorporating the decisions that turn us heavenward into our core values. Not just for the sake of the people who have advanced breast cancer, or require the warmth of human hands at St. Charles in Bend, but as a response to the needs of every employee who works with us.

How do we also serve the people who are well—and make them better? What do we have to offer, for everyone we come in contact with, that serves them as well as that box of Kleenex but has a little more substance?

I found an answer to that in a most curious way. And before I can explain, I need to tell you a story about our oldest daughter, Christa.

In the summer of 1989, I moved our family—including our two teenage daughters, Christa and Cara—from the suburbs of Vancouver, British Columbia, to Arlington, Virginia. I left a fantastic organization called Young Life, an international Christian ministry. Over the years, Young Life has crafted what I believe to this day is the most effective approach ever invented for introducing high school kids to the person and truth of Jesus Christ.

I had a new opportunity with a group of friends who help facilitate the National Prayer Breakfast, an annual gathering of national and international leaders that's held in Washington, D.C., in early February.

Christa had a new high school. Her mother and I probably survived the transcontinental journey better than she did. New friends didn't come all that easily for our daughter. As the weeks went by, she began to move in circles where a little drinking—wine coolers, I believe—and a few drugs were more generally accepted than they might have been at our house in Arlington.

65

I was gone the weekend in February when Christa came into our kitchen and told Carol, "Mom, I need to talk to you. I'm pregnant."

Carol and I were devastated. And our agonizing disappointment was only just beginning. As Carol once said, it was one wave after another, and our little stretch of beach really got pounded.

The first wave was the shattered dream, the swamping of

every sand castle we've ever built as parents. Then there was the tsunami of the boy's mother, who slapped some money down in front of Christa and said, "You get an abortion or I never want to see you again."

I don't think our daughter ever considered abortion. I don't know that she ever had big dreams; she was too fixed on the present, too fond of immediate gratification, to focus on the future. But she had a persistent sense of loyalty to the things she loved, a passion that she quickly extended to the life inside her. Even as Carol and I and a small army of friends and counselors were suggesting adoption, Christa decided she wanted to keep the baby.

She moved out of the house for a while. By Easter, she was living in an apartment with an unwed mother of a two-year-old. She was sleeping on the couch. It was a hectic scene. A lot of parties and wild nights. I think Christa was five months along when the phone rang and woke us at one-thirty in the morning. I could hear street traffic in the background. At that hour, you expect to hear a police officer or a coroner, but it was our teenage daughter, crying like a baby.

"I really want to come home," she said. "Will you come and get me?"

"You bet I will, sweetheart," I told her.

She was waiting on the apartment steps, next to a bag of her clothes. She was a mess. Christa got in the car and I hugged her really tight, and I said, "Honey, I'm so glad…I'm so glad you called."

67

She came home to live with us, even as more waves rolled in and broke upon our beach. Custody issues. Telling the grandparents. Sharing our disappointment and our new life with friends in the ministry. The phone call from the high school, telling us that Christa could graduate, but she would not be allowed to go through the proper ceremonies.

Christa said, "No, thank you." Instead, she went back to a little red schoolhouse, a halfway house, I suppose, for about twenty pregnant teenagers, one of whom was only thirteen years old. They'd converted the bedrooms into classrooms for the girls, one for English, one for typing, one for science. With the help of two wonderful mentors from Bell Atlantic, Christa stayed motivated and got her degree.

And in early October, Christa gave birth to a baby girl named Chelsea Ann.

If I ever needed proof that God doesn't make mistakes, it arrived in the form of that eight-pound girl. Christa was a single mother without a whole lot of training, so it made sense that she and Chelsea live with us for most of the next nine years. They saved money, and we had the joy of time with our daughter and a very special little child. All of which brings us to the summer of 1999.

Chelsea was eight years old. I was preparing to leave the house one morning, bound for a half-day presentation on leadership as part of the Rotary's Ryla training program at a place called Camp Menucah, when Carol said to me, "Honey, would you drop Chelsea off at the church?"

What a deal for me. Chelsea was pretty excited about a ride with Papa, so she jumped in the car and we headed up over the hill toward summer Bible school at this little Presbyterian church. On the way, Chelsea asked what I was doing that day, and I was just starting to explain the leadership conference when suddenly I had the strangest thought:

What does an eight-year-old girl think a leader is?

I don't know what I was expecting. Probably not a lot. After all, she hadn't read Bennis and the other books. She hadn't studied Churchill. Maybe I was hoping to get one of those cute little anecdotes that I could use in my opening remarks.

69

"Sweetheart," I said, "do you have any idea what a leader is?"

Ten short words. That's all. I only asked the question once. And I mean only once.

Chelsea didn't miss a beat. "Papa, you can trust a leader," she said. "And leaders always tell the truth."

Speaking of missing a beat...I think my heart skipped one. Here's my eight-year-old granddaughter, a raw rookie on the leadership speaking circuit, and she nailed it.

Trust? Stephen Covey calls it the "glue of life." It's the essential flux in any significant relationship, both in the workplace and where you live. And leadership, Walter Wright notes in *Relational Leadership,* "is a relationship of trust where commitments flow from character."

Leaders always tell the truth? This is basic too. Truth telling builds trust, and trust is the cornerstone of any healthy relationship. Consider the sins we forgive our friends—and, yes, even our children—if they are honest with us. Honesty is the baseline of any lasting relationship. Leaders generally keep their mouths shut so as not to inhibit the spontaneous energy in the room...but when they forget, they always speak the truth.

Chelsea, as you can see, was two for two. I was still doing the math when we pulled up to a red light at the top of the hill and Chelsea said, "Papa, if you're a leader, you obey the signs. Like 'Stop.'"

That's when I pulled over, right up against the curb, as soon as the light turned green.

That's when I grabbed the first piece of paper I could

reach—the map to Camp Menucah, I think it was—and began writing as fast as I could.

Why? Because everything Chelsea said was striking a nerve. Leadership, after all, is about building trust. Among its core values is truth telling. Those companies I spoke about back in the opening chapter? Global Crossing? Enron? Arthur Andersen? Many of their principals didn't tell the truth and didn't obey the basic rules of business.

71

A true leader knows how to read the signs and knows the importance of obeying them. Every business and organization has a vast array of red lights and green lights. We call them "policies" and "procedures."

Given that Chelsea was only eight years old, I knew she'd never read any corporate handbooks. I don't think she'd ever heard of photo radar. But she still knew—as a true leader would—that a red light is one of those signs we are obligated to obey.

If Chelsea had stopped there, I think I would have had a great story to take home to Carol. I would have had plenty of food for thought for the drive up the Columbia Gorge. But Chelsea was just getting warmed up.

"Papa," she said, "sometimes leaders have to do things that they don't like to do."

Of course they do. Trauma usually comes with the territory. Even if your company is a finely tuned machine, there will come a time when you have to deal with the fallout of a fallen world. People will show up with bad attitudes, the "I don't give a damns." They'll come to work late, misuse the equipment, or cut loose with unethical behavior that goes against the core values of the company.

Leadership demands that you respond. Some of your options may be unpleasant. Don't lead with your ego. Former President Dwight Eisenhower said it well: "You don't lead by hitting people over the head—that's assault, not leadership." We are called, instead, to confront the problem, not the personality, to sit down and go one-on-one with our coworker. Be relentless in seeking and speaking the truth. Look for an opportunity for growth.

Helen Keller, who never saw or heard a shadow or a whisper of a world that she understood better than most of us ever will, once said, "We could never learn to be brave and patient if there were only joy in the world."

Joy, the psalmist said, cometh in the morning, but the afternoons and evenings are often rife with disappointment, heartache, discipline, difficulty, and loss. That's the landscape a leader has to negotiate. The task list isn't always enviable or rewarding. You have to define reality even when the facts are unkind. You sometimes have to say thank you when your back is tired and your throat is dry. You have to step up and serve people when what you really need is a hot pad, a massage, and a bowl of chicken soup.

73

Sometimes leaders have to do things that they don't like to do. And each time you do, you gain courage and patience, at the very least.

I hope you can picture the two of us at the top of that hill, sitting in the car, the young girl focusing on the subject at hand, the old man—okay, not quite that old—scribbling as fast as he can. I think I was stretching my fingers when Chelsea said, "Papa, leaders always help people do their best."

And inside, I'm going, "YES! Yes, that's it! That's absolutely right." Tomorrow morning, leadership for each one of us will be looking at the people who work around us and helping them to do their best. Leadership isn't about a product. It's not about a process. It's not the product you deliver, but the people you deal with. Products and services can pay the bills, but people build the greatness in your organization. And you deal with those exasperating, troubled, but utterly human souls by encouraging them. Inspiring them. Doing your best, whatever it takes, to help them do their best.

Then Chelsea said, "If someone is hurting and you're a leader, you stop and help them."

That's Jim Lussier's message: We're caregivers. We're more than the hands on an assembly line; we're the hands that provide healing, compassion, assurance.

At the end of my visit to St. Charles Medical Center, Jim

took me downstairs to meet Sister Catherine, who is the last surviving nun from the group that founded the hospital. When Sister Catherine retired, Jim promised her that the hospital would take care of her for the rest of her life and begged her to come and go as she pleased. The hospital even bought her a house across the street.

Jim introduced us. She came out from behind her desk, a very small woman, simply and impeccably dressed, no makeup. I stuck out my hand. Sister Catherine took it in hers, and Jim began talking about our day together. After ten seconds or so, I realized Sister was still holding my hand.

Now, I don't know how many of you have ever held hands with a nun. I was a little uncomfortable. I wanted my hand back. I wanted it safe in my pocket. But Jim kept talking and Sister kept holding my hand, even as I had another thought: For fifty years, this woman has been holding the hands of people at the hospital who were falling apart or losing their grip.

That's what leaders do. "Leaders don't inflict pain," Max DePree said. "They bear pain." And my granddaughter had pounded another one into the bull's-eye: "If someone is hurting and you're a leader, you stop and help them."

By this time, that map to Camp Menucah was packed with scribbles. I had writer's cramp. And Chelsea was motoring right along. "If you're a leader, you share what you have with others," she said.

I said, "Honey, what do you mean by that?"

"Well, Papa, you know that Mommy and I fill up brown bags with old clothes and take them to Goodwill," Chelsea said. "And sometimes Mommy gives money to the church."

You share what you have with others. For our eight-year-old granddaughter, that was so basic, but I don't know that we all recognize the wisdom in that. All too often, the voice in our ear is whispering that we should hoard everything, locking it all away. In the business community, the most hideous theft is the hoarding of knowledge. Knowledge is power—and if you don't have the right relationships, employees often decide to stockpile that knowledge as a way of accumulating power. A company won't survive if all the knowledge is hidden away in silos instead of being shared openly.

On the personal level, I think we struggle to survive if we don't adopt a similar ethic, giving ourselves away whenever possible. I still remember attending a Special Olympics event at a Portland-area high school while Cara, our youngest daughter, was volunteering in special-ed classes.

77

At her urging, we were there to cheer Cara on as she helped a young girl who was both deaf and blind take part in the competition. It was amazing to watch Cara take the girl's hands in her own and sign directions and encouragement.

And I recalled that scene, years later, when I stood with Gene Nudleman at the Mt. Hood Kiwanis Camp for severely challenged young people and watched kids arrive for their long-anticipated week at camp. I had tears in my eyes watching parents say good-bye to the sons and daughters who were utterly dependent on others for their well being. Entrusting their children to the camp, safe as it was, took courage.

There were poignant moments at the Kiwanis camp, most of which were delivered by the board members and support staff on hand to make sure these kids had the time of their lives. That isn't always easy. Some of the children have unusual responses, or none at all. They require extra measures of patience. But when you step up to meet that requirement, you experience unconditional giving at its best.

78 All of this came back to me, mind you, while my granddaughter Chelsea shared her wisdom and her heart.

Chelsea then said this: "If you're a leader, Papa, and something is poison, you tell people."

As you might imagine, I was wondering where that came from. So I asked her. And Chelsea said, "You know. Mommy told me there are bottles underneath the sink that I should never, ever touch."

Lysol. Comet. 409. Soft Scrub. Hey, there are a lot of bottles under there that I never, ever touch either. If you drink the stuff, you're history.

But one of the functions of a leader is to create a safe place for the people you work with. I'm not talking about a panic room, a remote hideaway to which you can flee in some dire emergency. I'm talking about a safe harbor, a sanctuary from the chop through which all of us maneuver.

Not long ago, I spoke to a woman named Barbara, who had just moved on to a new career after several years as the executive assistant to the CEO of a publicly traded company based in Portland. She moved on, Barbara said, because she would come to work on Monday mornings and by noon, she would feel half an inch tall. She was whittled down by the destructive, humiliating, and manipulative culture inside the building.

The language was crude. The voices were angry. People only had value in that world if they didn't complain while you put your foot on their throat and crawled over them on their way to the top.

No one deserves that kind of work environment. I'm convinced that so many of us have a TGIF perspective because Mondays fill us with dread. There's no mystery why there are more heart attacks on Mondays than any other day of the week. Yet we would, I believe, count Monday as a blessing if the workplace were a safe harbor for us and a sanctuary we could extend to others.

As a leader, you obviously want to create a place that is safe physically. But you also want to create a place that is safe intellectually, where people are encouraged to be creative and to bring ideas forward that—regardless of their merits—won't be met with ridicule.

You also want to create a place that is safe emotionally. A place where someone like Faye can wear her red wig and break down now and then.

And finally, you want to create space that is safe spiritually. Where faith can be expressed and, I might add, a lack of faith is unchallenged.

Chelsea? She closed with a flourish. "Papa," she said, "you know, if you make a mistake and you're a leader, you say 'Sorry.'"

"Leaders always say 'Thank you.'"

And you know what? Leaders don't say either one of those things via e-mail. E-mail is both convenient and immediate, but an e-mail doesn't arrive with the warmth of a hand-written note.

It isn't as intimate as the loops and spirals of a person's handwriting.

81

And it all too quickly disappears into the empty ether of the Internet. Handwritten notes have staying power. They're usually tucked away into the top desk drawer, where you can pull them out a month or two later and savor them all over again. When you write those thank-you notes, I'm a big fan of sending them home so that the family and friends of the person you are celebrating can peek at the note and recognize the value this man or woman brings to the company. Apologies and thank-you notes aren't the stuff of performance reviews and strategic plans, but they are essential in building the human side of any organization.

Chelsea had two final suggestions.

"If you're a leader, you're a good sport," she said. "You're not a quitter."

As I've thought over the years about our talk that morning, I'd like to think Chelsea learned that from her mother. Christa never gave up on her dreams, on the importance of finishing school, on following through with her pregnancy, on her own daughter. I'm reminded of two of my favorite quotes from Winston Churchill. You probably remember the first:

> *Never give in! Never give in! Never, never, never, never—in nothing, great or small, large or petty—never give in except to convictions of honour and good sense.*

But I also love this one:

> *Success is the ability to go from failure to failure without losing your enthusiasm.*

Enthusiasm, you see, is contagious. It's the life jacket that keeps you afloat while the waves of failure are rolling over you. It's the optimism that eliminates quitting from your list of options.

At the very end, Chelsea said this: "A leader always says 'Good job.'"

I can promise you this: By the time she was eight years old, *83* our granddaughter had probably read Sandra Boynton and the Berenstain Bears. She'd undoubtedly curled up with the Narnia tales or the books of Laura Ingalls Wilder at one time or another. But she'd never read Max DePree. And yet, amazingly enough, they'd ended up at the same place:

The first responsibility of a leader is to define reality. The last is to say thank you. In between the two…

Well, not quite the same place.

DePree, you recall, takes all this one step farther.

CHAPTER 6

Legacy

*One thing I know: The only ones among you
who will be really happy are those who will
have sought and found how to serve.*

ALBERT SCHWEITZER

*The greatest among you
shall become your servant.*

JESUS OF NAZARETH

I n between the two?

"In between the two," Max DePree argues, "the leader
must become a servant."

And what does that mean? Almost every definition I know
pales beside the example of a woman named Linda Gilleese.

Linda has lived in the town of Hermiston, on the banks of the Columbia River in Oregon, her entire life. She's the daughter of a farmer and the mother of seven kids. She's been a den mother, a 4-H leader, a religious-ed instructor. She managed the Umatilla County Fair for five years, served on the school board for sixteen and worked at the blood bank for forty.

And what brings her to mind when I think about those who have sought and found how to serve is a comment that was made about Linda when she was introduced at the 2002 White Rose Luncheon, a March of Dimes benefit that honors Oregon's most dynamic women.

A friend offered a tribute to Linda's work ethic. As busy as Linda was, her friend said, she had never heard her complain that someone else wasn't doing his or her fair share.

Think about that for a moment. She had never heard Linda complain that someone else wasn't doing his or her fair share. Why? Because Linda doesn't divide the things that need to be done into her share and the obligation of others. Instead, she stretches to fill the gap. She steps up and fills the void.

She answers the question Francis Schaeffer once asked: "How shall we then live?"

You want to lead? You have to serve. The formula isn't all that complicated.

You don't need a title. You simply must act, as Linda Gilleese does, out of an inspirational, empathetic set of core values. And if you want your company to follow your lead, you must create and nurture a culture in which those same values flourish. You don't need hierarchal control if everyone believes the same things and aspires to the same things.

Are you looking for guidelines on being a servant first? I think Robert Greenleaf got us started when he said the following:

> *The servant-leader is servant first. It begins with the natural feeling that one wants to serve. Then conscious choice brings one to aspire to lead. The best test is: do those who I serve grow as persons; do they while being served become healthier, wiser, freer, more autonomous, more likely themselves to become servants?*

Put yourself to the test. Do those I serve grow as people? Do they become healthier, wiser, freer...and more empowered?

Do I create a safe place for those who work with me?

Do I understand what makes people who they are and how they think and react in different situations? Knowing a soft answer turns away wrath, do I take the time to listen?

Do I throw light or cast a shadow?

Do my words match up with my touch? Do the people I serve trust that I believe in them...and believe that I trust them?

Do I let other people take the credit and receive the prize?

Do I keep my promises?

And do I offer forgiveness when mistakes are made, or do I hold people hostage?

I have a wonderful friend named Bob Farrell, who started Farrell's Ice Cream Parlours and four other restaurant chains. I think Bob opened 133 ice-cream stores over the years. Not a single one ever failed. And the key to that success wasn't the ice cream. True, there was a rumor going around that Bob had a secret formula for that ice cream, a recipe he snuck out of the Bronx.

No, Farrell's ice cream was the same Tillamook brand you could buy down at Safeway. His chocolate syrup arrived in the traditional Hershey's can. His bananas were…well, normal bananas.

Truth is, you didn't go to Farrell's for the ice cream. You went there for the experience. And that experience was framed by the core values of Bob Farrell and his company and animated by employees who knew they were utterly and completely cared for.

Small wonder. I once asked Bob to define leadership for me. His comeback was stark and unforgettable: "Take care of your people," he said. "Take care of your customers."

Bob once commissioned a customer service survey in which he discovered that 68 percent of the customers who decide not to frequent a business don't return because they dislike the attitude of indifference in the staff.

People recognize, relate to, and respond to the values of a company. They are attracted by them or repelled by them.

And that's where leadership comes in. Management focuses on accomplishing a task. Leadership is about building the human side of organizations. For far too many years, the emphasis in the business community has been misdirected. At Norpac, we know how to handle orders. We know how to shift large quantities of frozen vegetables from one part of the globe to another. Where we need help is in encouraging people inside the organization to get along with each other. In developing the healthy relationships that actually facilitate tackling the task at hand. In learning every day to serve each other enthusiastically.

I think it helps when a company spells out its core values, committing them to paper. Over the last several years, I've been fortunate to work with a company that's done just that—Auto-Owners Insurance. Auto-Owners was founded in Mount Pleasant, Michigan, in 1916. They've made an investment in teaching and promoting their core values because they want them to permeate their corporate culture, including the 5,500 agencies and 35,000 independent insurance agents with whom they have a covenant.

One of those values is to make a profit. They have zero debt. They own all their own real estate outright. That's a commitment they've made: to be profitable. To the delight of their employees, they're also committed to sharing that profit with their people.

The core values at Auto-Owners Insurance are spelled out in a booklet called *The Fisherman*. Among the values that "make up the heart of Auto-Owners Insurance" are honesty, hard work, prudence, and loyalty.

Are the folks at Auto-Owners getting a little soft?

Absolutely. "Leaders focus on the soft stuff," Tom Peters wrote in "Rule #3: Leadership Is Confusing as Hell":

People. Values. Character. Commitment. A cause. All
of the stuff that was supposed to be too goo-goo to

*count in business. Yet, it's the stuff that real leaders
take care of first. And forever. That's why leadership is
an art, not a science.*

I remember when Richard Rieten, a friend and the CEO of
NW Natural Gas in Portland, Oregon, leaned across a board-
room table and said to me, "Great companies are built out of
the soft stuff."

What did he mean by "soft"? What do we mean by "soft"?
We don't mean the fluff. We don't mean mushy, wishy-
washy, or unsubstantial. Instead, think of "soft" in the
context of the "soft hands" you might hear about with a top
basketball prospect.

What does it mean when a young talent is described as having the "softest hands you've ever seen"? It means he catches
everything thrown his way. He never drops the ball. He
swallows other guys' mistakes. When a bad shot or a
rebound or a turnover ends up in his hands, it is transformed into something marvelous and productive: A quick
two points. A brilliant outlet pass. The initial surge in a
game-winning rally.

First, I think leadership is character. Character is a word that comes from the Greek "engraved." It's from the French "inscribed." It isn't just a superficial style. It's got to do with who we are as human beings and what shapes us.

■ WARREN BENNIS

Far too many people turn cold and hard on their way up the corporate ladder. They grow up and grow old thinking that the incentive to arrive at the top is to reach a position where you command the most people. The CEOs and CFOs that Arianna Huffington so aptly describes in *Pigs at the Trough* decided that the employees, the shareholders, and those handy pension funds were there to serve them. They didn't experience the radical change of heart that transformed Jim Lussier at the crossroad in his life, when he realized he was meant to serve, not be served.

Does that sound like an impossible dream? Does service sound like a burden, a doubling of your workload, an unfathomable forfeiture of time?

Or is there a reason no one has ever heard Linda Gilleese

93

complain? Is it possible that when you stop fastidiously dividing the workload into your portion and the obligation of others, you might inspire others to do the same?

When leaders surrender to the idea of being a servant, they aren't giving away the farm. They are increasing the number of people who are invested in the harvest.

94 "With great power comes great responsibility."

Do you remember who said that? Was it Winston Churchill? Tom Peters? Ronald Reagan?

Nope. Stan Lee, one of the creative minds behind the boom at Marvel Comics in the early 1960s. Lee slipped those words to Spider-Man forty years ago, and they still ring true today.

Consider this: If you share the power, you share the responsibility. If you provide everyone with the power to influence the course of your company, you invest everyone with the stake of responsibility and set them free to serve.

Leadership is not reserved for the CEO. The underwriter, the sales clerk, the schoolteacher, the administrative assistant, the janitor, why even the eight-year-old girl inspiring her Papa at a traffic light, have the same opportunity on a daily basis when they bring everything they are—the "whole person" that Henry Ford cared so little about—to their career and their community.

When they value relationships. When they bring dignity and respect to conversations. When they rise to serve their boss, their peers, the policy holder, and the customer.

When their life on the outside reflects what stirs and motivates them on the inside.

When, regardless of what it says on their name tag, they understand their *real* job description:

Caregiver.

I don't know how many of you know American Sign Language, which transforms thoughts into the music of your hands.

I'm told there's a significant difference between the signs for management and leadership. "Management" begins with three fingers of the right hand touching the shoulder, where the epaulets on a military uniform sit. You then bring the right hand down and the left hand up and take hold of a set of reins, as if you were controlling a horse.

"Leadership"? The one hand begins at the heart, then drops down to take hold of the other hand, as if you were guiding another person along. Hand in hand.

There's a lot to be said for hands, for offering them, for holding them. In the aftermath of my colon surgery, I went on a wild, unexpected journey that included twenty-four weeks of chemotherapy at Kaiser Oncology in north Portland. To facilitate the placement of the needle that supplied those drugs, the nurses at Kaiser would put a hot plastic pack on top of my hand to warm up the skin and bring out the veins. As soon as that hot pack did the trick, the nurses would give me the plastic pack to grip as they slid the needle in.

That procedure changed very subtly when a nurse named

Belynda showed up after several weeks. When she removed the hot pack from my hand, she tossed it in the garbage.

Then she gave me her hand to grip as she went hunting for that vein.

Her hand wasn't significantly warmer. It wasn't quite as pliable as that damp plastic. But what a world of difference it made. Instead of gripping a shroud, I was embracing life. When I took Belynda's hand, I was pulled toward the light.

97

Belynda later told me that the nurses had handcrafted a motto that was meant to guide in those situations:

"Lifting spirits. Touching lives."

You want a definition for leadership? We might as well end there. When I was holding Sister Catherine's hand back at St. Charles, she said this to me about Jim Lussier: "He is a leader who is not concerned about how many followers he has. He is a leader who creates leaders."

If you truly want to lead—and which of us is called to do

anything less?—you are in the business of lifting spirits and touching lives.

Each time you put your hands to that good work, you *redefine* reality.

You say thank you.

98 You become a servant.

And one thing more: You put your vision for leadership into the hands of someone else and send them off to serve in the worlds beyond your reach.

Special Thanks

___

We stand so tall because we stand on
the shoulders of those who have gone before us.
WINSTON CHURCHILL

This is an impossible task, but I will try!

First, to Carol Ann, my wife of thirty-eight years and the personal embodiment of the greatness found in leadership. Thanks for knowing me better than I know myself. You were right: I did have something to say about leadership.

I have had the extraordinary privilege of being in the company of leaders throughout my life: watching, listening, questioning, laughing, crying, and celebrating together.

It was Dr. M. L. Custis who met with me every Wednesday throughout the four turbulent years of college. A mentor before the term became fashionable. In gratitude and in memoriam.

Neal Arntson, you "lifted" when I was leaning. I wouldn't be where I am today without you. You are a hero!

Bob Farrell, you have been my cheerleader every day, including this one. A heart of thanks!

For my early lessons in leadership, I owe a debt of thanks to the men and women of Young Life. Their strength, passion, and commitment over the twenty-four years we worked together both in the United States and Canada changed my life. *Merci beaucoup!*

I remain particularly inspired by the people who serve at the YMCA, the Kiwanis' Mt. Hood Camp for severely challenged young people, the Rotary, and Ryla. You are giants in the community!

For the business associates and friends who have dared to share their personal leadership journey with me over the years, I am grateful. In these upside-down, stressed-out times we live in, you have been generous with your time, wisdom, and friendship. You men and women are giants!

Early morning dialogue, midday scrutiny, and late-night deliberations turned into a renewed friendship with a man whose hunger and passion for writing gave structure and meaning to my own enthusiasm for this book. Steve Duin's gift for expression, his desire to "get it right," and his integrity born of the heart have made this journey one for which I will always be grateful. Steve, my friend, thank you very much!

A personal note of thanks to a circle of friends who always believed, who offered insight and counsel, who read and re-read early drafts, made suggestions, inspired me to keep going, prayed, and offered their shoulders. My deep appreciation goes to Rick and Joan Malouf, Dr. Peter Legge, Roger Looyenga, Dr. Angus Gunn, Jerry Carlson, Marshall Christensen, Scott Melrose, David King, Denny Walter, John Davies, and Dick Wingard.

For all of you: We did this together.

Two Kinds of People

There are two kinds of people
On earth today.
Just two kinds of people
On earth, I say.
Not the rich and the poor
For to know a man's wealth
You must first know the state
Of his conscience and health,
Not the happy and sad,
For in life's passing years
Each has his laughter
And each has his tears.
No, the two kinds of people
On earth I mean,
Are the people who lift
And the people who lean...

ELLA WHEELER WILCOX, POET AND JOURNALIST
(1850–1919)

The LORD upholds all who fall
and lifts up all who are bowed down.
—PSALM 145:14, NIV

Additional Reading on Leadership

The mere brute pleasure of reading...
the sort of pleasure a cow must have in grazing.

G. K. CHESTERTON

Bennis, Warren. *Managing People Is Like Herding Cats* (Executive Excellence, 1997).

Blanchard, Ken. *The Heart of a Leader* (Honor Books, 1998).

————. *Mission Possible: Becoming a World-Class Organization While There's Still Time* (McGraw-Hill, 1996).

Burns, James MacGregor. *Transforming Leadership: The Pursuit of Happiness* (Atlantic Monthly Press, 2003).

DePree, Max. *Leadership is an Art* (Currency, 1989).

———. *Leadership Jazz* (Currency, 1992).

Gardner, John W. *On Leadership* (Free Press, 1989).

Gerber, Robin. *Leadership the Eleanor Roosevelt Way: Timeless Strategies from the First Lady of Courage* (Prentice Hall, 2002).

Greenleaf, Robert. *Servant Leadership: A Journey into the Nature of Legitimate Power and Greatness* (Paulist Press, 2002).

Jaworski, Joseph. *Synchronicity—The Inner Path of Leadership* (Berrett-Koehler, 1996).

Koestenbaum, Peter. *Leadership—The Inner Side of Greatness* (Jossey-Bass, 2002).

Lipman-Blumen, Jean. *Connective Leadership: Managing in a Changing World* (Oxford University Press, 2000).

Lowney, Chris. *Heroic Leadership: Best Practices from a 450-Year-Old Company That Changed the World* (Loyola Press, 2003).

McGinnis, Alan Loy. *Bringing Out the Best in People* (Augburg Press, 1985).

Phillips, Donald T. *The Founding Fathers on Leadership: Classic Teamwork in Changing Times* (Warner Books, 1997). *107*

Waitley, Denis. *Empires of the Mind* (William Morrow, 1996).

Willingham, Ron. *The People Principle: A Revolutionary Redefinition of Leadership* (Diane Publishing, 1997).

Wright, Walter. *Relational Leadership* (Paternoster Publishing, 2000).

The Holy Bible, New Testament.

To contact the author...

With the same passion, practicality, and gift of storytelling that he brought to this book, Chuck Ferguson can inspire leadership in your conference, seminar, sales meeting, or retreat with a dynamic, energetic presentation.

Chuck brings international experience to the task: He taught the inaugural class on leadership development at the Kazakh-American Free University in Kazakhstan, courtesy of the Marshall Christensen Foundation.

Chuck would love to hear from you about how this book has affected you or your organization. Share your leadership stories, insights, and experiences, and he will respond to you with a personal note.

You can contact Chuck
through the 21st Leadership Group
at P.O. Box 82033, Portland, Oregon 97282-0033;
phone (503) 699-3312; fax (503) 699-0869.
His e-mail address is cfergusonleader@yahoo.com.

LEADERS
SHED LIGHT

Don Neraas